Love Letters in the Sand

Love Letters in the Sand

The Love Poems of
KHALIL GIBRAN

CALLIGRAPHY BY
Lassaâd Metoui

PREFACE BY
Malek Chebel

SOUVENIR PRESS

First published in Great Britain in 2005
by Souvenir Press
43 Great Russell Street London WC1B 3PD

This book is based on *Lorsque l'amour vous fait signe... suivez-le*
Published in France by Editions Lattès

ISBN 0 285 63721 5

Typeset by FiSH Books, London
Printed in Great Britain by the University Press, Cambridge

For…

A…

Beauty's Messenger

Love is a harmonic that speaks uniquely to the heart that has learned to hear it. Better attuned than others to its resonances, however deep and intimate they are, this singular heart is the most acutely aware of the other's music, but is also the most fragile.

'A fragile heart, an agile heart' goes the old French adage. And if this heart knows how to capture another's music, and fervently cherish and nurture it, whether in a gilded cage or in completely voluntary subjection, it would indeed be a bad heart, were it no longer receptive to it.

Such is the exacting love of the poet, love that cannot exist without passion.

Among all the exponents of Arab aestheticism in France in our time, the troubadour Lassaâd Metoui is one of the best interpreters.

In calligraphing the emotions that feed our everyday sensibilities, the artist spreads his canvas, dips his quill in beauty's conch and shares with us that subliminal approach which is at the heart of the mystery of Arab letters, the mystery of writing.

Malek Chebel

The springtime
of love

When love beckons to you, follow him,

Though his ways are hard and steep.

And when his wings enfold you, yield to him,

Though the sword hidden among his pinions may

wound you.

And when he speaks to you,

believe in him.

Though his voice may shatter your dreams

as the north wind lays waste the garden.

For even as love crowns you so shall he crucify you.
Even as he is for your growth so is he for your pruning.
Even as he ascends to your height and caresses your
tenderest branches that quiver in the sun,
So shall he descend to your roots and shake them
in their clinging to the earth.
Like sheaves of corn he gathers you unto himself.
He threshes you to make you naked.
He sifts you to free you from your husks.
He grinds you to whiteness.
He kneads you until you are pliant;
And then he assigns you to his sacred fire, that you may
become sacred bread for God's sacred feast.

All these things shall love do unto you that you may
know the secrets of your heart, and in that
knowledge become a fragment of Life's heart.

But if in your fear you would seek only love's peace
and love's pleasure.

Then it is better for you that you cover your
nakedness and pass out of love's threshing-floor,

Into the seasonless world where you shall laugh, but
not all of your laughter, and weep, but not all of
your tears.

Love has no other desire but to fulfil itself.

But if you love and must needs have desires, let
these be your desires:

To melt and be like a running brook that sings its
melody to the night.

To know the pain of too much tenderness.

To be wounded by your own understanding of love;

And to bleed willingly and joyfully.

To wake at dawn with a winged heart and give
thanks for another day of loving;

To rest at the noon hour and meditate love's ecstasy;

To return home at eventide with gratitude;

And then to sleep with a prayer for the beloved in
your heart and a song of praise upon your lips.

Love one another,
but make not a bond of love:
Let it rather be a moving sea between
the shores of
your souls.

Darkness may hide the trees
and the flowers from the eyes
but it cannot hide
love from the soul.

Every human being can desire,
and desire, and desire still more,
until that desire tears away the veil
of appearances covering his eyes,
and he can finally see his essence.
He will then be able to see
the abstract substance of life.
For all essence is the abstract
substance of life.

Who would sell me one beautiful thought
for a hundred pounds of gold? Who
would exchange one minute of love
for a handful of gems?
Who would give me one eye
that can see beauty,
in exchange for all my treasures?

Life without Love is like a tree barren of
blossom and fruit. And Love without Beauty is
like flowers without scent and fruits
without seeds...Life, Love, and Beauty
are one independent and absolute trinity,
which cannot be separated or changed.

If sorrow does not carry you
in her womb, if despair does not
feel pain in giving birth to you,
and if love does not bring you
into this world in its cradle of dreams,
your whole life
remains a blank page in the book
of the universe.

True beauty is a ray
   That springs from the sacred depths of the soul,
    and illuminates the body, just as life
      springs from the kernel of a stone and
       gives colour and scent to a flower.

It is a perfect understanding
   between a man and a woman. And it happens
   in the blinking of an eye. This affinity
   is born in a single moment, and is greater
   than all other affinities, this spiritual
   conversion we call: Love.

*None can reach dawn
without travelling the road
of night.*

The autumn
of love

And in the autumn, when you gather
  the grapes of your vineyards for the winepress,
   say in your heart,
    'I too am a vineyard, and my fruit
    shall be gathered for the winepress,
    And like new wine I shall be kept
    in eternal vessels.'

And your fragrance shall be my breath,
And together we shall rejoice through
all the seasons.

For love that seeks aught
    but the disclosure of its own mystery
    is not love but a net cast forth:
    and only the unprofitable is caught.

For to be idle is to become a stranger
unto the seasons, and to step out
of life's procession
that marches in majesty and
proud submission
towards the infinite.

Love is

quivering happiness.

The sorrow of love sings,
  The sorrow of knowledge speaks,
   The sorrow of desire whispers,
    And the sorrow of poverty weeps.
    But there exists a sorrow deeper
     than love, more noble than knowledge,
     stronger than desire, and more bitter
     than poverty.
   This sorrow has no voice, it is dumb,
  but its eyes glitter like the stars.

Strange, the desire
for certain pleasures
is a part of my pain.

And when my Joy was born

And when my Joy was born, I held it in
  my arms and stood on the house-top shouting,
  'Come ye, my neighbours, come and see,
  for Joy this day is born unto me.
  Come and behold this gladsome thing
  that laugheth in the sun.'

  But none of my neighbours came to look upon
  my Joy,
and great was my astonishment.

And every day for seven moons
  I proclaimed my Joy from the house-top –
and yet no one heeded me.
And my Joy and I were alone,

unsought and unvisited.

Then my Joy grew pale and weary
because no other heart but mine
held its loveliness and no other
lips kissed its lips.

Then my Joy died of isolation.

And now I only remember
my dead Joy in remembering
my dead Sorrow. But memory
is an autumn leaf that murmurs
a while in the wind and then
is heard no more.

Life kisses our faces
every morning. Yet,
between morning and evening,
she laughs at our sorrows.

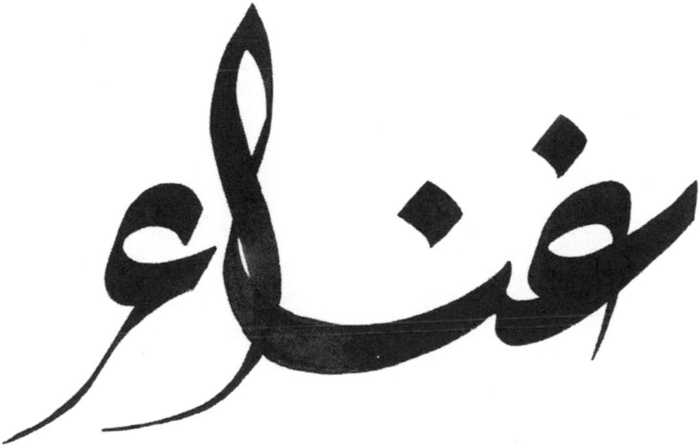
غناء

Hearts united in pain and sorrow
will not be separated by joy and happiness.
Bonds that are woven in sadness
are stronger than the ties of joy and pleasure.
Love that is washed by tears
will remain eternally pure and beautiful.

Love is a deadly poison injected by
 black vipers, who writhe in the caves
  of Hell. The poison flows there,
   spreads, and falls like dew.
   Thirsty souls drink it.
   And are intoxicated for a minute,
   sober again for a year,
   then dead for a century long.

The feelings we live through
in love and in loneliness
are simply, for us,
what high tide
and low tide are to the sea.

For life goes not backward
nor tarries with yesterday

The sorrowful spirit finds peace in solitude
and isolation. So she flees mankind
like the wounded gazelle who leaves
the herd, and hides in her cave,
until either she heals or she dies.

Man clings to substantial things,
  as cold as ice, while I seek the flame
  in my belly. Since I have discovered
  that substantial things deaden
  a man, painlessly,
  while love awakens him
  to life and suffering.

I want to die from longing, and never
 live in boredom. I want there to be,
  in the depth of my soul,
   a hunger for love and beauty.
   As I observe mankind, I see
    that those who are satisfied are the most
     wretched, and the most attached to matter.
     I have also heard the sighs of those
    who are full of desire and longing
   and have found in them a gentleness
 sweeter than the sweetest melody.

Love is a thick mist that surrounds the soul
on every side, and hides the secret of
existence from it, so that it sees only
the shadows of its desires
trembling among the rocks,
and hears only the echo of its cries
from the empty valley.

الفصول

Sorrow is just a wall

between two gardens.

The summer
of love

Love gives naught but itself
and takes naught
but from itself.
Love possesses not
nor would it be possessed.

When you part from your friend,

you grieve not;

For that which you love most in him

may be clearer in his absence,

as the mountain to the climber

is clearer from the plain.

Love is a word of light,
  written by a hand of light,
  upon a page of light.

Narrow-minded love
seeks to possess
the beloved.
But boundless love
is never so demanding.

The great longing

Here I sit between my brother the mountain
  And my sister the sea.

  We three are one in
    loneliness, and the love that binds us together
    is deep and strong and strange.
    Nay, it is deeper than
    my sister's depth and stronger
    than my brother's strength, and stranger
    than the strangeness of my madness.

  Aeons upon aeons have passed since
    the first grey dawn made us
    visible to one another; and though we have
    seen the birth and the fullness and the death
    of many worlds, we are still
  eager and young.

We are young and eager and yet
we are mateless and unvisited, and though

we lie in unbroken half embrace,
we are uncomforted.
And what comfort is there for controlled desire
and unspent passion? Whence shall come the flaming
god to warm my sister's bed?
And what she-torrent shall
quench my brother's fire? And who is
the woman that shall command my heart?

In the stillness of the night my sister
murmurs in her sleep the fire-god's
unknown name, and my brother calls afar
upon the cool and distant goddess.
But upon whom I call in my sleep
I know not.

Here I sit between my brother
the mountain and my sister the sea. We three
are one in loneliness, and the love
that binds us together is deep and strong
and strange.

The heart, with its ramified feelings,
  is like a cedar with spreading branches.
   If the cedar lose a strong branch,
    it suffers, but does not die,
    it carries its vital energy
    to the neighbouring branch,
    that will grow and fill the void
    with its young green twigs.

Love is the only freedom
 in this world. Because it elevates
  the spirit to such a supreme point
  that neither mankind's laws
   nor its customs can touch it,
   nor can the laws or facts of
   nature change its course.

They say: 'If a man
 knew himself,
  he would know all mankind.'
  I say: 'If a man loved
  mankind, he would know
  something of himself.'

You are free before the sun of the day,
and free before the stars of the night;

And you are free when there is no sun
and no moon and no star.

You are even free when you close
your eyes upon all there is.

Love letters in the sand

When love beckons to you...follow it

Silence

The springtime of love

Melody

Spiritual

One minute of love

The springtime of love

Feelings

Dance

Eternal

Dreams

 Light

 Day

 Love is quivering happiness

 Hope

 The act is the image of love

 Patience

 Tenderness

 Beauty

 Hear

Love letters in the sand

 Value

 Revelation

 Singing

 Secrets

 Absolute

 Friend

 Sincerity

 The Seasons

 Desire

 Voices

Perfume

 Sun

 Path

 My soul

 Sorrow

 Wind

 Life goes not backward nor tarries with yesterday

 The path

 The veil of desire

 Space